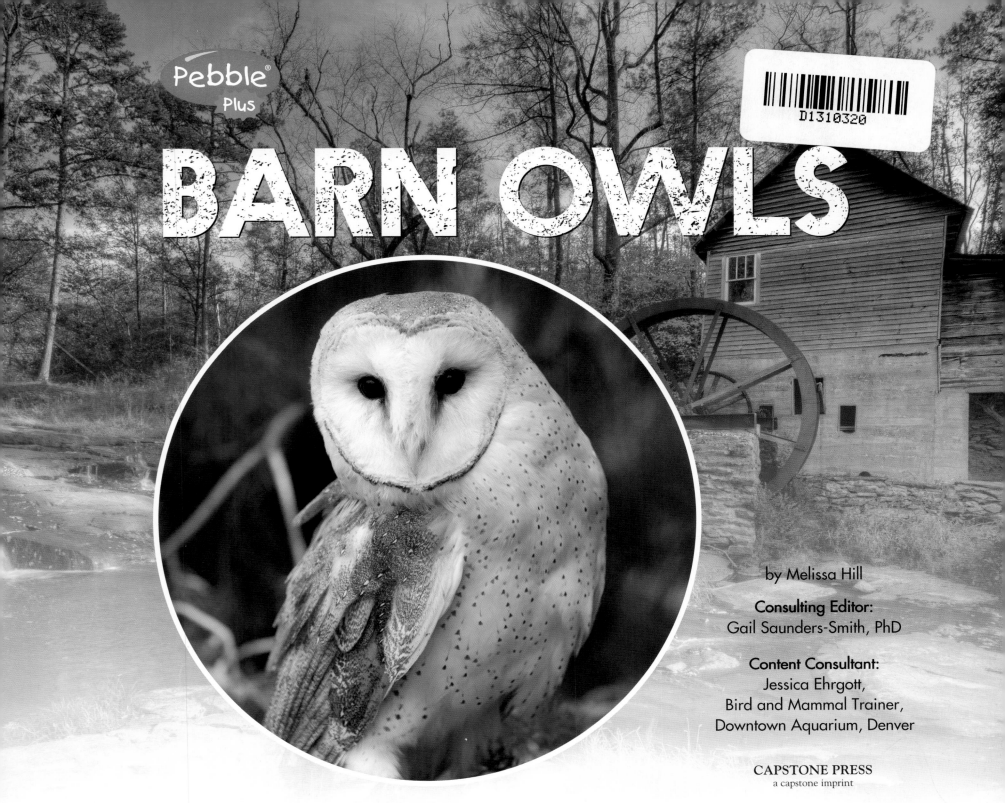

Pebble Plus

BARN OWLS

by Melissa Hill

Consulting Editor:
Gail Saunders-Smith, PhD

Content Consultant:
Jessica Ehrgott,
Bird and Mammal Trainer,
Downtown Aquarium, Denver

CAPSTONE PRESS
a capstone imprint

Pebble Plus is published by Capstone Press,
1710 Roe Crest Drive, North Mankato, Minnesota 56003
www.capstonepub.com

Library of Congress Cataloging-in-Publication Data
Hill, Melissa, 1975- author.
Barn owls / by Melissa Hill.
pages cm.—(Pebble Plus. Owls)
Summary: "Simple text and full-color photographs describe
barn owls"—Provided by publisher.
Audience: Ages 5–8.
Audience: K to grade 3.
Includes bibliographical references and index.
ISBN 978-1-4914-6045-0 (library binding)
ISBN 978-1-4914-6051-1 (paperback)
ISBN 978-1-4914-6065-8 (eBook pdf)
1. Barn owl—Juvenile literature. I. Title.
QL696.S85H55 2015
598.9'7—dc23   2015005324

Editorial Credits
Jeni Wittrock, editor; Juliette Peters, designer; Morgan Walters, media researcher;
Katy LaVigne, production specialist

Photo Credits
Dreamstime: Steve Allen, 17; Getty Images: Berndt Fischer, 11, Steve Maslowski, 19; Glow
Images: Manfred Danegger/Corbis, 15; iStockphoto: iculizard, 21; Shutterstock: Andrew
Astbury, 7, Artography, (mossy bark) cover and throughout, Artography, (red bark texture)
background 3, Dennis W. Donohue, inset 1, 9, Eric Isselee, (parakeet) bottom right 10, (barn
owl) backcover, bottom left 10, J. Helgason, (tree stump) back cover, 2, 24, jadimages, 13, John
C Evans, (owl perched) bottom left 3, Patrick Rolands, 22, Philip Ellard, cover, Sean Pavone,
(lanscape gristmill) back cover, 1, 2, 23, 24, Stawek, (map) 8, Valerio Pardi, 5

Note to Parents and Teachers

The Owls set supports national curriculum standards for science related to life
science. This book describes and illustrates barn owls. The images support
early readers in understanding the text. The repetition of words and phrases
helps early readers learn new words. This book also introduces early readers to
subject-specific vocabulary words, which are defined in the Glossary section. Early
readers may need assistance to read some words and to use the Table of Contents,
Glossary, Read More, Internet Sites, Critical Thinking Using the Common Core,
and Index sections of the book.

Printed in China by Nordica
0415/CA21500542
042015   008837NORDF15

Table of Contents

Shriek
in the Night

Hiss! What was that? It was a barn owl. Barn owls don't hoot like other owls do. These pale owls shriek and hiss.

Worldly Owls

Barn owls live near open fields and deserts. They're often found inside empty buildings, like barns. That's how they got their name.

Barn owls are rarely seen during the day. But they live all over the world. Barn owls live on every continent but Antarctica.

Barn Owl Range Map

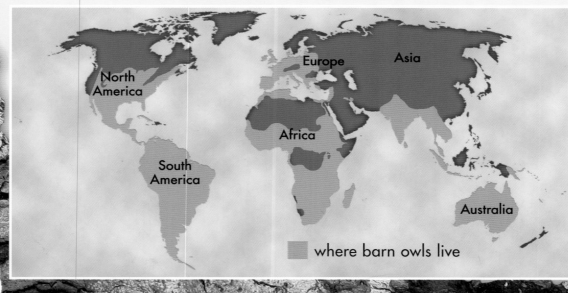

North America

Europe

Asia

Africa

South America

Australia

where barn owls live

Hungry Hunters

Barn owls are raptors.

These flying hunters weigh

1 pound (0.5 kilogram).

Their wings stretch out

about 3.5 feet (1.1 meters).

Size Comparison

barn owl
length:
13–16 inches
(33–41 centimeters)

parakeet
length:
6–8 inches
(15–20 centimeters)

Barn owls are nocturnal.
In the dark they hunt prey
by listening. Their heart-shaped
faces catch sounds made by
small animals.

An owl flies toward the sound
of its prey. His long legs
stretch out. He grabs
the mouse with his talons.

A barn owl can eat 1,000 mice in a year. They also eat other rodents, rabbits, and small birds. In the wild, barn owls can live 10 years or more.

Family to Feed

Barn owls need to be good hunters. They have large families to feed! They may have as many as nine chicks each year.

After two months, barn owl

chicks can fly. Soon they

will be hunting too.

Small animals, look out!

GLOSSARY

continent—one of Earth's seven large land masses

hiss—to make a "sss" sound like a snake

nocturnal—to be active at night and rest during the day

predator—an animal that hunts other animals for food

prey—an animal that is hunted by other animals for food

raptor—a bird of prey that hunts and eats other animals, catching them with their feet

rodent—one of a group of small mammals with large front teeth for chewing

shriek—a high scream or call

talon—a long, sharp, curved claw

READ MORE

Bodden, Valerie. *Owls.* Amazing Animals. Mankato, Minn.: Creative Paperbacks, 2014.

Marsh, Laura. *Owls.* National Geographic Readers. Washington, D.C.: National Geographic, 2014.

Rissman, Rebecca. *Barn Owls: Nocturnal Hunters.* Read and Learn. Chicago: Heinemann Library, 2015.

INTERNET SITES

FactHound offers a safe, fun way to find Internet sites related to this book. All of the sites on FactHound have been researched by our staff.

Here's all you do:

Visit *www.facthound.com*

Type in this code: 9781491460450

Super-cool stuff!

Check out projects, games and lots more at
www.capstonekids.com

CRITICAL THINKING USING THE COMMON CORE

1. Barn owls live 10 years in the wild. Why might barn owls live longer in a zoo or raptor center? (Integration of Knowledge and Ideas)

2. Owls are raptors. Raptors are birds that catch prey using their feet. What other birds might be raptors? (Integration of Knowledge and Ideas)

INDEX

Word Count: 202
Grade: 1
Early-Intervention Level: 16